DRUMS

CD INCLUDED

HAL•LEONARD
BIG BAND
PLAY-ALONG
VOLUME 1

Swing Favorites

ISBN-13: 978-1-4234-2216-6

HAL•LEONARD®
CORPORATION
7777 W. BLUEMOUND RD. P.O. BOX 13819 MILWAUKEE, WI 53213

Visit Hal Leonard Online at
www.halleonard.com

4

This page intentionally left blank

As recorded on NICE 'N' EASY
april in paris

Words by E.Y. HARBURG
Music by VERNON DUKE
Arranged by DAVE BARDUHN

I'VE GOT YOU UNDER MY SKIN

Words and Music by
COLE PORTER
Arranged by JOHN BERRY

DRUMS

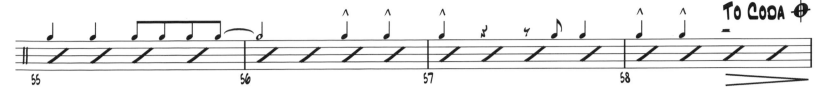

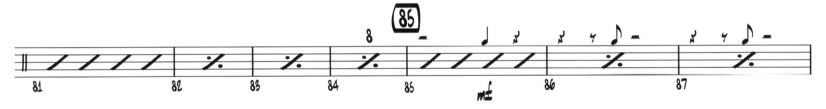

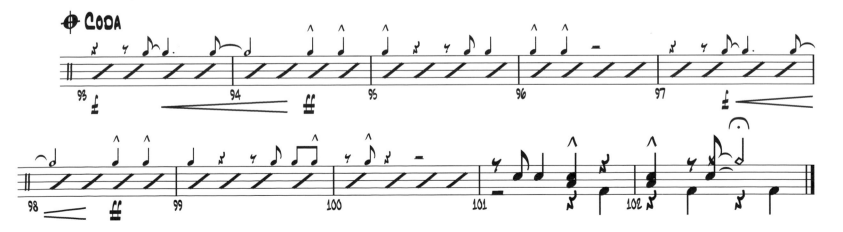

IN THE MOOD

Words and Music by JOE GARLAND
Arranged by PAUL LAVENDER

DRUMS

It Don't Mean a Thing
(IF IT AIN'T GOT THAT SWING)

DRUMS

Words and Music by
DUKE ELLINGTON and IRVING MILLS
Arranged by MARK TAYLOR

Recorded by THE BRIAN SETZER ORCHESTRA

ROUTE 66

By BOBBY TROUP
Arranged by PETER BLAIR

DRUMS

DRUMS

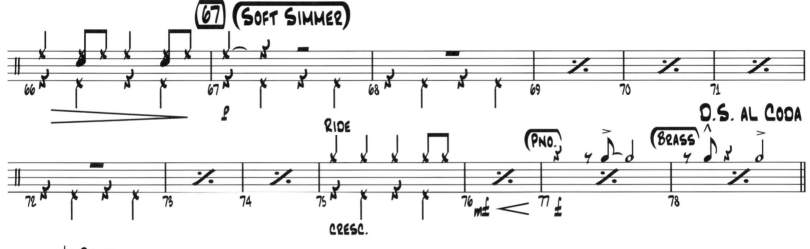

SPEAK LOW

Words by OGDEN NASH
Music by KURT WEILL
Arranged by MARK TAYLOR

Drums

STOMPIN' AT THE SAVOY

Recorded by BENNY GOODMAN

By BENNY GOODMAN,
EDGAR SAMPSON and CHICK WEBB
Arranged by DAVE BARDUHN

From the Paramount Picture THE FLEET'S IN

TANGERINE

DRUMS

Words by JOHNNY MERCER
Music by VICTOR SCHERTZINGER
Arranged by JOHN BERRY

DRUMS

From THE BOYS FROM SYRACUSE

THIS CAN'T BE LOVE

Words by LORENZ HART
Music by RICHARD RODGERS
Arranged by MARK TAYLOR

DRUMS

DRUMS

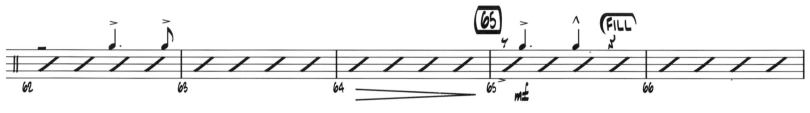

D.S. AL CODA

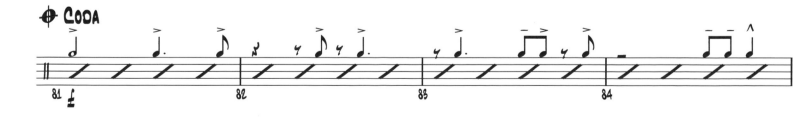

CODA

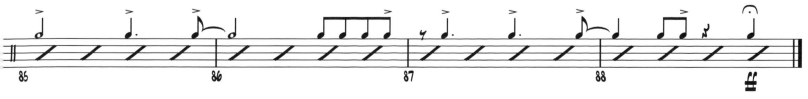

UNTIL I MET YOU
(Corner Pocket)

By FREDDIE GREEN and DON WOLF
Arranged by MARK TAYLOR

Drums

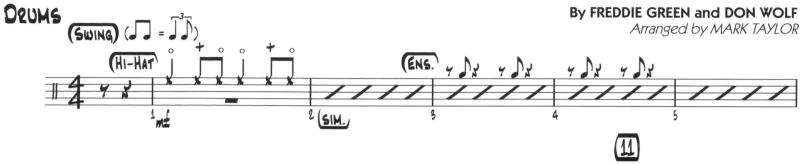

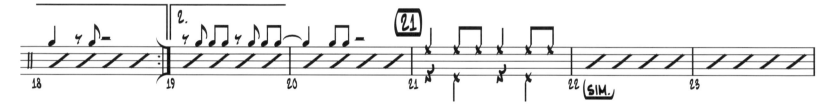

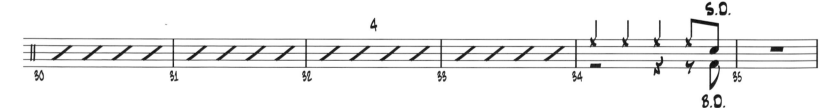

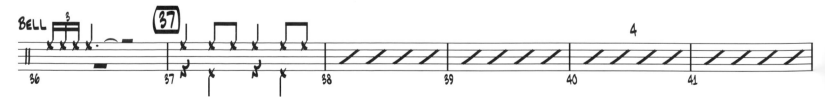

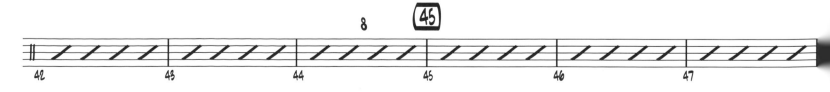

Drums